Published By Robert Corbin

@ Joe Goins

Self-discipline: Mastering the Art of Self-control for Lasting Achievement

All Right RESERVED

ISBN 978-87-94477-81-9

TABLE OF CONTENTS

Chapter 1 1

Mastering Self-Discipline: The Foundation Of Lasting Success 1

Chapter 2 26

Understanding Self-Discipline 26

Chapter 3 48

Understanding The Self 48

Exploring Personal Values: Navigating The Compass Of Self-Identity 48

Chapter 4 53

What Does Mental Toughness Actually Entail? 53

Chapter 5 61

Getting Started 61

Chapter 6 65

Keys To Self-Discipline 65

Understanding The Essence Of Self-Control 67

Chapter 7 75

Why You Need To Be Self-Disciplined 75

Chapter 8 84

The Disciplined Mindset 84

Chapter 9 91

The Psychology Of Self-Discipline 91

Chapter 10 98

The Principles Of Self-Discipline 98

Chapter 11 106

Conquer Your Mind, Conquer The World 106

Chapter 12 124

The Self-Discipline Framework 124

Developing A Unique Framework 124

Chapter 13 133

Mastering Self-Discipline: The Foundation Of Lasting Success 133

Chapter 14 157

Emotional Intelligence 157

CHAPTER 1

MASTERING SELF-DISCIPLINE: THE FOUNDATION OF LASTING SUCCESS

Understanding Self-Discipline: More than Just Willpower

Imagine standing at the base of a majestic mountain. Its towering peak pierces the sky, and the path leading to the summit is filled with challenges: sharp rocks, treacherous turns, and steep inclines. Now, imagine two climbers. The first is filled with fiery passion and a burst of motivation to reach the peak. He starts quickly, driven by his excitement, but his energy quickly fades. After a short distance, he feels overwhelmed and decides that the climb is too difficult, and he abandons his quest.

The second climber, on the other hand, approaches the mountain with a calm determination. He has prepared both mentally and physically for the climb, understanding that it won't be easy. Each step is measured, and when he encounters obstacles, he pauses, reassesses, and finds a way forward. His journey is not fueled by mere momentary motivation but by a deep-rooted discipline that keeps him going, step by step, until he finally stands victorious at the summit.

In life, it is this enduring self-discipline that propels us forward. Willpower may ignite the initial spark, but without discipline, the journey is seldom completed. So let us cultivate discipline; let us be the second climber, who triumphs in the face of challenges and reaches new heights.

The Misconception of Willpower

In the popular imagination, willpower is often viewed as the ultimate determinant of those who achieve their goals and resist distractions or temptations. We've all heard phrases like, It's a matter of willpower, or, If only I had more willpower. This kind of thinking attributes a substantial portion of our success or failure in various endeavors, be it dieting, studying, or even saving money, to this singular, mysterious force. But is willpower truly the key? And if so, how does it operate? Let's explore the intricate dynamics surrounding willpower, its limitations, and the broader spectrum of factors that influence self-control.

Defining Willpower: A Comprehensive Perspective

Before delving deeper into the concept of willpower, it is essential to clarify that it plays a vital role in regulating our impulses, emotions, desires, and actions. Our ability to delay gratification, resist temptations, and pursue long-term goals, even when immediate rewards beckon, depends on it.

Its strength goes beyond mere determination. It's a complex interplay of various factors like cognitive abilities, emotional intelligence, energy levels, motivation, habitual patterns, and the cultural context. Mastering each of these dimensions can set the stage for significant breakthroughs in personal growth and attainment.

The Finite Model of Willpower

Willpower, in recent scientific studies, has been likened to a finite resource, similar to a muscle that can tire out after intense exertion. Similarly, our willpower can wane after periods of sustained mental effort or resistance to temptation, a phenomenon called ego depletion.

For instance, in a well-known experiment, participants who restrained themselves from the temptation of freshly baked cookies, subsequently showed reduced persistence in solving challenging puzzles. Their previous act of restraint had, it seems, drained their willpower. This example leads to a glucose-depletion effect, where glucose, a primary source of energy for the brain, decreased as participants exerted self-control.

What's fascinating is that this depletion seems to have a biological correlate. As participants exerted self-control, their glucose – a primary source of energy for the brain – levels decreased. When they replenished their glucose, their willpower also appeared to be restored. Moreover, glucose's role is significant but more nuanced, intertwined with our beliefs about willpower, motivations, and overall physiological state. Therefore, simply downing a sugar-laden drink won't instantly supercharge one's willpower.

Beyond the Finite Model: Mindset, Motivation, and Other Elements

The muscle analogy and glucose observation are compelling, but they are only parts of a complex picture. Other research suggests that our beliefs about willpower can shape its reality, where those who perceive willpower as an inexhaustible resource tend to exhibit more stamina while requiring self-control than those who see it as finite. Additionally, motivation plays a colossal role, where pushing through even when our willpower reserves seem low becomes more attainable if the reasons for a task align deeply with our values or when there's substantial intrinsic motivation.

Moreover, while willpower is undoubtedly a crucial player in self-control, it doesn't operate in isolation. Several other elements come into play:

Habits: Once a behavior becomes habitual, it requires significantly less willpower. For example, someone who has cultivated the habit of running every morning might do so with little to no conscious effort.

Environment: Our surroundings have a profound effect on our behavior. A clutter-free workspace might enhance productivity, while a kitchen stocked with unhealthy snacks can thwart dieting efforts.

Support Systems: Having a support system, be it friends, family, or support groups, can act as external enforcers of discipline.

Mindset: A growth mindset, where challenges are seen as opportunities for growth rather than threats, can make perseverance more natural.

Rest and Recovery: Just as with physical exercise, periods of rest allow for the recovery of willpower. Sleep, relaxation, and leisure are vital.

Strategies for Enhancing Willpower

Given its importance and the challenges in maintaining it, are there ways to enhance our willpower? Yes, and they often lie in addressing the broader ecosystem of self-control.

Regularly challenge yourself: Much like a muscle, regular challenges, even small ones, can help in bolstering willpower.

Mindful practices: Activities like meditation can increase self-awareness, allowing for better impulse control.

Positive visualization: Visualizing the benefits of achieving a goal can provide a boost when willpower wanes.

Avoid decision fatigue: Reduce trivial decisions to preserve willpower for more critical tasks. For example, having a set routine or a predetermined menu can help.

In conclusion, understanding the intricacies of willpower, addressing the vast array of other factors at play, and taking the necessary steps to enhance it through a holistic approach may offer a more comprehensive perspective towards achieving greater success.

The Misconception of Willpower: A New Perspective

As we have seen therefore, recent research has shown that relying solely on willpower is like sprinting in a marathon race. Just as our physical energy diminishes, so does our willpower when continually taxed. Therefore, it is crucial to understand what makes up the fabric of self-discipline.

The Pillars of Self-Discipline

If we can't solely rely on willpower, what then makes up the fabric of self-discipline? Here are the integral pillars:

Awareness: The cornerstone of discipline is understanding one's strengths, weaknesses, desires, and triggers. Being acutely aware allows one to preempt challenges and strategize effectively.

Consistency: Unlike the sporadic nature of willpower, consistency ensures that actions become habits. It's not about monumental changes but small, daily actions that culminate in success.

Resilience: Discipline involves facing setbacks head-on and having the fortitude to bounce back, learning from each experience.

Prioritization: Not every task demands your attention. Knowing what aligns with your goals and dedicating time and effort to them is pivotal.

Delayed Gratification: At its core, discipline is about forgoing immediate pleasures for long-term gains. It's the ability to see beyond the present moment and work towards a future reward.

Harnessing the Power of Habit

Habits aren't just actions, as Charles Duhigg says in his renowned book The Power of Habit, but cycles that start with a cue, which leads to a routine and culminates in a reward. Understanding and manipulating this cycle is crucial in fostering discipline. A particular habit ingrained in our routine no longer relies on willpower; instead, it becomes a part of our muscle memory. For example, consider a practiced pianist. Their fingers glide over the keys, not because of daily bouts of motivation, but because disciplined practice has ingrained the movements into their very being.

The Path Ahead

The subsequent chapters offer a more detailed exploration of self-discipline, from its psychological foundations to its practical applications. Discipline is not about being stringent or restrictive; it is about harnessing an internal power, channeling it effectively, and cultivating a life where dreams are attainable realities. Understanding the terrain is the first step towards transforming your life with self-discipline.

The Impact of Self-Discipline on Life Success

There is a prevalent belief in our society that natural talent, luck, or even socioeconomic background are the predominant factors in achieving success. Despite the common perception, self-discipline is often the determining factor for long-term success. Self-discipline acts as a rudder in the vast ocean of life, allowing individuals to navigate storms, avoid pitfalls, and steer towards their desired destination.

The Domino Effect of Discipline

Imagine a line of dominoes. The act of pushing just one can set off a cascade, resulting in a spectacular display. Similarly, one disciplined action in life can trigger a series of beneficial events, creating an upward spiral of positive outcomes. For example, a commitment to waking up early can lead to a more productive morning routine, allowing for focused work, regular exercise, and a balanced breakfast. This series of disciplined actions contributes to better mental clarity, improved health, and enhanced overall well-being.

In other words, contrary to popular belief, success isn't always achieved through monumental decisions or grand gestures. Instead, it's a culmination of numerous small choices made through consistent, disciplined actions. These choices compound over time, leading to significant life successes.

Discipline as a Bridge to Turning Dreams into Reality

Everyone has dreams. But without discipline, dreams often remain just that - intangible and unrealized. By consistently applying effort towards achieving goals, individuals can turn their dreams into reality. For example:

Career Advancement: Those with discipline often stand out in the workplace. Their dedication to tasks, time management, and continual learning make them valuable assets, leading to opportunities for advancement and growth.

Health and Fitness: Disciplined habits such as balanced nutrition, regular exercise, and adequate sleep translate to robust health, reduced illness, and greater longevity.

Financial Security: Discipline in financial management, which includes saving, investing wisely, and curbing impulse purchases, paves the way for a stable financial future.

Creating Strong Relationships through Discipline

At a glance, discipline might seem unrelated to interpersonal relationships. However, a deeper look reveals its profound impact. By practicing self-discipline, individuals cultivate qualities like patience, active listening, and commitment, which strengthen bonds, build trust, and nurture enduring personal and professional relationships.

The Long-Term Vision

Through deliberate, disciplined growth, individuals can witness profound transformations in both their internal and external lives within a year. Mapping out a clear plan for the year, with quarterly reviews, monthly focus areas, weekly check-ins, and daily habits, provides the foundation for success. Consistent effort, embracing challenges, building a support system, documenting the journey, and celebrating milestones, no matter how small, are key in achieving a year of transformation.

Self-discipline promotes a forward-thinking mindset. Rather than being swept up in the immediacy of life's daily grind, disciplined individuals keep their eyes on the horizon. They set long-term goals and chart out pathways to reach them. This vision not only guides their current actions but also instills a sense of purpose and direction in life. With the tools of self-discipline in hand, individuals are poised to take on any journey, one day at a time, and achieve greatness.

The Journey Ahead: One Year of Dedicated Transformation

The ticking of a clock, the turning of calendar pages, the changing of seasons—time is ceaseless in its march. Yet, how we choose to utilize this time can drastically alter its significance in our lives. By dedicating ourselves to transformation, significant changes can be achieved in just one year, both internally and externally. This guide presents a clear path to deliberate and disciplined growth.

Creating a 365-Day Blueprint

Before beginning any journey, it's essential to have a clear plan. Breaking the year down into quarterly reviews, monthly focus areas, weekly check-ins, and daily habits ensures progress towards your goals.

This doesn't mean plotting out every single day to the last detail, but rather setting clear milestones and objectives. In the next chapters we will see together how to do it.

The Power of Consistency

In a world obsessed with overnight successes, the quiet power of consistency often goes unnoticed. Yet, it's in the daily grind, the unwavering commitment to the task at hand, that true transformation lies. Within a year, consistent effort can yield astounding results, from mastering a new skill to achieving a long-desired goal.

Embracing Challenges

Obstacles during your transformational journey are inevitable. There will be days of doubt, moments of weakness, and periods of stagnation. However, by facing these challenges head-on, you can grow both personally and professionally, furthering your progress and fortifying your character.

Building a Support System

Nobody can achieve their goals alone. Surrounding yourself with communities and mentors who align with your vision can prove invaluable in providing support, guidance, and shared experiences that can be invaluable.

Remember, the power of collective energy and wisdom can significantly amplify individual efforts.

Documenting the Journey

Maintaining a journal or log of your progress offers a tangible record of achievements, while also serving as a motivator on days when your motivation wavers. Revisiting your documented journey can reignite the spark and remind you of how far you've come.

Celebrating Milestones, No Matter How Small

Acknowledging and cherishing every small triumph in your expedition can serve as a catalyst to propel you towards future successes. This gesture of recognition not only elevates your spirits quintessentially but also instills an unwavering drive to face any trials ahead.

The recognition and celebration of minor achievements play a critical role in the pursuit of larger goals. Often, we overlook the smaller milestones along the way. However, these seemingly insignificant accomplishments form the bedrock of ultimate success, and their acknowledgment can serve as a powerful motivator. Every grand journey is made up of countless small steps. When we take the time to acknowledge each of these steps, we not only validate the hard work involved but also create a reinforcing loop. This affirmation boosts our self-confidence, reminding us of our capabilities and the progress we've made so far.

Furthermore, it helps to cultivate a mindset of gratitude and positivity. This attitude fosters resilience, particularly during challenging times when larger goals seem elusive. These moments of recognition provide mini-respites, allowing us to recharge and push forward with renewed vigor.

Consistently noting and celebrating minor accomplishments also creates a record of success over time. Reflecting on this growing list of achievements can provide the encouragement needed to overcome obstacles, ensuring that we remain motivated and committed to our overarching objectives. In essence, the recognition of small victories is not just a nod to the past but a potent catalyst for future endeavors.

In Conclusion

We often underestimate what we can do in a year. Through disciplined action, unwavering commitment, and a clear vision, 365 days can morph into a transformative expedition, reshaping the contours of one's life.

With this potential, it's a journey worth embarking upon. As the year begins, take up the challenge of crafting your masterpiece, one day at a time.

Importantly, while January is typically associated with new beginnings, personal growth and transformation aren't restricted to the start of the year. Any point on the calendar can be the perfect time to embark on a journey of self-improvement. This guide offers monthly reflections and exercises to aid you on your path, but don't be afraid to customize them to fit your unique story. However, adhering to the recommended order will provide structure for those seeking guidance. Remember, having a roadmap - even if you diverge from it at times - is better than navigating solely by intuition.

CHAPTER 2

UNDERSTANDING SELF-DISCIPLINE

You can never conquer the mountain. You can only conquer yourself.– Jim Whittaker, American mountaineer and CEO

Marietta wakes up before dawn each morning to exercise. She works very efficiently in the office, ignoring distractions, and devoting all of her attention to high-value projects. In the evening, she attends a class online; she'll be graduating in a few months with her MBA.

How can people like Marietta achieve so much, so consistently? And how can we accomplish as much in our personal lives and careers? Part of the answer lies in self-discipline. This is what pushes us to deliver on our best intentions and goals, even when we don't feel like doing so. If we have self-discipline, we're able to put off short-term pleasure (or endure short-term inconvenience or discomfort) in the pursuit of long-term gain.

This is why self-discipline is so important. In this article, we'll examine what self-discipline is, we'll explore why it's useful, and we'll look at how to develop it.

A Definition of Self-Discipline

Self-discipline is the ability to push yourself forward, stay motivated, and take action, regardless of how you're feeling, physically or emotionally. You're showing it when you intentionally choose to pursue something better for yourself, and you do it despite factors such as distractions, hard work, or unfavorable odds. Self-discipline is different from self-motivation or willpower. Motivation and willpower contribute to it, as do persistence, the ability to follow through on your intentions, and hard work.

Learning to effectively lead yourself and others all comes down to discipline. Happiness, success, and fulfillment stem from focus and self-control. It may be hard to believe when you're facing an all-you-can-eat buffet, the prospect of making a quick buck, or the lazy lure of sleeping in versus getting on the Peloton, but studies show that people with self-discipline are happier. Why? Because with discipline and self-control, we accomplish more of the goals we truly care about. Self-discipline is the bridge between goals defined and goals accomplished.

You have power over your mind—not outside events. Realize this, and you will find strength. ~ MARCUS AURELIUS

There are specific strategies you can execute to learn self-discipline and gain the willpower to live a happier, more fulfilling life. If you are looking to take control of your habits and choices, here are the eight most powerful things you can do to master self-discipline—which is imperative for life beyond your comfort zone—and maybe even redefine extraordinary.

Know your strengths and weaknesses .

We all have weaknesses. Whether they're the desire for alcohol, tobacco, unhealthy food, obsession over social media, or the video game Fortnite (what the heck is with this game by the way?!), they have a similar effect on us. Weaknesses don't just come in the form of areas where we lack self-control either. We all have our strong suits and the stuff we kind of stink at. For example, I don't care about having difficult conversations, lengthy paperwork that involves digging up old documents I never saved in the first place, holding my temper when someone is shooting at me, or calling into automated phone systems.

And therefore, I used to actively (or purposefully) avoid these activities. Now, I strive to tackle them head-on—or I delegate them to others. (Never forget about the subtle art of delegation!)

Self-awareness is a powerful tool for comfort zone expansion, but it requires constant focus and acknowledging your shortcomings, whatever they may be. I suffered from bad allergies and asthma growing up and had terrible eyesight. Those were some significant weaknesses when considering becoming a Navy SEAL. But so what? I trained hard to improve my lung function and used the money I'd saved for LASIK eye surgery.

Too often people either try to pretend their vulnerabilities don't exist or they succumb to them with a fixed mindset, throwing their hands up in defeat and saying, Oh well. Know your strengths, but more importantly, own up to your flaws. You can't overcome them until you do.

Remove temptations.

I can resist anything except temptation. ~ OSCAR WILDE . As the saying goes, Out of sight, out of mind. It may seem silly, but this phrase offers powerful advice. By simply removing the biggest temptations from your environment, you will greatly improve your self-discipline. When I decided I was going to pursue the lofty goal of becoming a SEAL, everything in my life had to change. If you want to eat healthier, toss the junk food in the trash. Want to drink less? Throw out the booze. If you want to enhance your productivity at work, improve the management of your To-Do's, turn off social media notifications, and silence your cell phone. Prioritize and execute.
The fewer distractions you have, the more focused you will be on accomplishing your goals.

Set yourself up for success by ditching bad influences.

Set clear goals and have an execution plan.
If you hope to achieve greater degrees of self-discipline, you must have a clear vision of what you hope to accomplish, just like any goal. You must also have an understanding of what success means to you. After all, you don't know where you are going, it's easy to lose your way or get sidetracked. Remember to prioritize.
A clear plan outlines each time-bound step you must take to reach your goals. Create a mantra to keep yourself focused. Successful people use this technique to stay on track, emotionally connect to their mission, and establish a clear finish line.

Practice daily diligence.
We aren't born with self-discipline; it's a learned behavior. And just like any other skill you want to master, it requires daily practice and repetition. It must become habitual. But the effort and focus

that self-discipline requires can be draining. As time passes, it can become more and more difficult to keep your willpower in check. The bigger the temptation or decision, the more challenging it can feel to tackle other tasks that also require self-control.So, work on building your self-discipline through daily diligence in a given area associated with a goal. This goes back to step three. To practice daily diligence, you must have a plan. Put it on your calendar, or your to-do list, tattoo it on the back of your eyelids - whatever works best for you. With practice, anyone can push the boundaries of their comfort zone every day.

Create new habits and rituals.

Acquiring self-discipline and working to instill a new habit can feel daunting at first, especially if you focus on the entire task at hand. To avoid feeling intimidated, keep it simple. Break your goal into small, doable steps. Instead of trying to change everything at once, focus on doing one thing consistently and master self-discipline with that goal in mind.

As we say in the SEAL Teams, Eat the elephant one bite at a time.

If you're trying to get in shape but don't exercise regularly (or ever), start by working out ten or fifteen minutes a day. If you're trying to achieve better sleep habits, start by going to bed thirty minutes earlier each night. If you want to eat healthier, change your grocery shopping habits and prep meals ahead of time. Take baby steps. Eventually, when your mindset and behavior start to shift, you can add more goals to your list.

Change your perception of willpower.

If you believe you have a limited amount of willpower, you probably won't surpass those limits. As I mentioned previously, studies show that willpower can deplete over time. But what about changing that perception? The SEAL candidate who believes they probably won't make it through training won't succeed. Why assume our will to win can only take us so far? When we embrace the mindset of unlimited willpower, we continue to grow, achieve more, and develop mental toughness. It's the same philosophy as setting stretch goals. In short, our internal conceptions about willpower and self-control can determine how disciplined we are. If you can remove these subconscious obstacles and truly believe you can do it, then you will give yourself an extra boost of motivation toward making those goals a reality.

Let's say you aspire to become a trapeze expert but tell yourself, Well, I'm probably not going to excel at this, so chances are I'll be sticking with miniature golf.

That's a lame backup plan wrapped in mediocrity. We are talking about contingencies for intentional course correction, not planning for failure.

So be bold and keep moving forward. Going in with a plan will help give you the mindset and self-control necessary for the situation. You will also save energy by not having to make a sudden decision based on your emotional state.

Find trusted coaches or mentors.

The development of expertise requires coaches who are capable of giving constructive, even painful, feedback. Real experts are extremely motivated students who seek out such feedback. They're also skilled at understanding when and if a coach or mentor's advice doesn't work for them.

The elite performers I've known and worked with always knew what they were doing right while concentrating on what they were doing wrong. They deliberately picked unsentimental coaches who would challenge them and drive them to higher levels of performance.

The best coaches also identify aspects of your performance that will need to be improved at your next level of skill and aid you in preparation.

Forgive yourself and move forward.

Even with all our best intentions and well-laid plans, we sometimes fall short. It happens. You will have ups and downs, great successes, and dismal failures. The key is to keep going. A very close SEAL buddy of mine has had a lifelong dream of not just serving in the SEAL Teams but also making it to our tier-one special missions unit. He has every qualification this unit could want, but for some reason, they didn't select him on his first application attempt. Did he wallow in sorrow? Not for one second. He immediately developed a plan to request even more schools, train even harder, and he transferred to a different SEAL Team for a better chance to get picked up next time. Easy day.

If you stumble, find the root cause by asking the five WHYs and move on. Don't let yourself get wrapped up in guilt, anger, or frustration, because these emotions will only drag you further down and impede future progress.
Learn from your missteps and forgive yourself. Then get your head back in the game and violently execute. Good luck!
Understanding the path to achieving goals requires recognizing the profound significance of self-discipline.
From maintaining healthy habits and managing time effectively to enhancing productivity *and* fostering personal growth, self-discipline is the

cornerstone that supports the architecture of success.

However, many individuals grapple with a lack of self-discipline.

This can lead to procrastination, impulsive decisions, and detrimental habits that impede progress and growth. It can affect personal and professional life, causing missed opportunities and unfulfilled potential.To move from aspiration to achievement, it's important to build and practice self-discipline.

A person who has mastered self-discipline can overcome the lure of immediate gratification in pursuit of long-term goals, which is a key trait of successful people.

Moreover, self-discipline plays a crucial role in time management and eliminating procrastination. By training yourself to focus on your tasks and responsibilities, you can resist distractions and delay gratification, reducing procrastination significantly. This increased productivity can lead to improved performance, whether in your studies, work, or personal projects.

Additionally, self-discipline has a positive impact on mental health and overall well-being. Discipline can reduce stress and tension as it promotes a sense of self-control and direction. It fosters resilience and determination, fortifying mental and emotional health.

How to build self-discipline

Building self-discipline is a journey, not a destination. It's about making a conscious effort to improve each day, acknowledging setbacks as part of the process, and celebrating small victories. While the path to self-discipline can be challenging, the rewards are well worth the effort and struggle.

Ways to build self-discipline

Start small

Building self-discipline can be an overwhelming task if approached all at once. Begin by setting small, achievable goals. This could be as simple as waking up ten minutes earlier each day or committing to a daily 15-minute workout.Achieving these goals can create a sense of accomplishment and boost your confidence in your ability to exercise discipline. Self-discipline is doing what needs to be done — even when you don't feel like it.

Eliminate bad habits

Habits, especially detrimental ones, play a significant role in our lives and can often undermine self-discipline. Start by identifying your bad habits — perhaps excessive social media browsing, unhealthy snacking, or procrastination. Once identified, work on strategies to eliminate them. This could involve setting specific rules (such as no social media during work hours), using apps that track or limit the habit, or substituting the bad habit with a more positive one.

Develop good habits

On the flip side, creating and maintaining good habits can substantially boost self-discipline. Incorporate healthy routines into your daily life, like regular exercise, reading, or practicing mindfulness.

An effective approach is to employ the principles outlined in James Clear's book Atomic Habits. Clear emphasizes the importance of making small changes that add up to significant results over time. A practice as simple as keeping a water bottle at your desk to increase water intake, or reading a page of a book each night before sleep, can make a big difference in the long run.

Practice self-control

Self-control is the foundation of self-discipline. Increasing self-control can help reduce impulsivity, making it easier to stick to your goals and avoid distractions.

Practical tips to enhance self-control include techniques like the pause and plan strategy where, when faced with a decision, you take a moment to reflect on the outcomes before acting.

Mindfulness practices can also enhance self-control by promoting greater self-awareness. Tools such as meditation apps or guided breathing exercises can help cultivate mindfulness

Exercise regularly

Regular physical exercise is not just a boon to your health; it also fosters discipline. The commitment to a consistent workout schedule necessitates self-control and determination, key components of self-discipline.

Exercise also generates a sense of accomplishment that can spill over into other areas of your life, promoting the creation of new habits and the achievement of small goals.

Establish a specific goal-setting process
Self-discipline thrives on a clear vision. Setting short-term and long-term goals provides direction and focus. Ensure your goals are specific, measurable, achievable, relevant, and time-bound (SMART) to make them effective.

Short-term goals can act as stepping stones towards your long-term objectives, breaking them down into manageable chunks, which makes the process less daunting and more achievable.

Step out of your comfort zone

Self-discipline involves regularly pushing beyond your comfort zone. Facing new challenges or trying unfamiliar tasks can bolster your mental fortitude and adaptability.

Whether it's public speaking, learning a new skill, or taking on additional responsibilities at work, stepping out of your comfort zone promotes growth and enhances discipline.

Limit social media and junk food

Minimizing distractions and unhealthy choices is essential for self-regulation, an integral part of self-discipline. Spending excessive time on social media can lead to procrastination and time mismanagement.

Likewise, frequent consumption of junk food can impact your physical well-being and weaken your self-control. Establish boundaries on social media use and opt for healthier food alternatives to support your self-disciplined journey.

Practice self-awareness

Self-awareness is the foundation of self-discipline. Being cognizant of your strengths, weaknesses, and triggers can guide your behavior and decision-making.

Regular introspection or practices like journaling can help you better understand your patterns and reactions, enabling you to make conscious changes that strengthen your self-discipline.

Use apps and tools

Technology can be a powerful ally in your quest for self-discipline. Time management apps can help you track and manage your time better, while to-do list tools can assist in organizing and prioritizing tasks.

LinkedIn can be used for professional growth and networking, keeping you focused on your career goals. Podcasts offer a wealth of knowledge and motivational content for self-improvement and discipline.

Additionally, habit-tracking apps can help you establish and maintain good habits.

Building self-discipline is a gradual process, demanding sustained effort and the capacity to navigate various hurdles. Chief among these obstacles are perfectionism and the fear of failure.

Inculcating self-discipline means accepting that mistakes and setbacks are inherent components of the journey, not detours. They're opportunities to learn, refine, and grow. Instead of striving for unreachable perfection, it's more pragmatic and productive to aim for continuous progress.

Using affirmations . Affirmations can be a crucial tool in combating negative self-talk, a main roadblock in the path to self-discipline.

Crafting positive self-dialogue and practicing affirmations can operate as a quick pick-me-up and help foster a positive growth mindset. This mindset encourages a belief in your potential to improve, amplifies resilience, and sustains motivation even in challenging times.

CHAPTER 3

UNDERSTANDING THE SELF

EXPLORING PERSONAL VALUES: NAVIGATING THE COMPASS OF SELF-IDENTITY

In the tapestry of our lives, personal values serve as the threads that weave the fabric of our character. They are the guiding principles, the moral compass that directs our decisions, shapes our relationships, and defines the essence of who we are. Embarking on the journey of exploring personal values is akin to navigating the intricate landscape of self-identity, unraveling the layers that make us unique.

Identifying Core Values

At the heart of this exploration lies the task of identifying our core values—those fundamental beliefs that resonate deeply within us. What principles do we hold dear, even when faced with the ebb and flow of external influences? This section invites you to introspect, to sift through the myriad values that may have shaped you, and to discern the ones that form the bedrock of your authentic self.

Aligning Actions with Values

Identifying values is only the beginning; the true power lies in aligning our actions with these principles. This segment encourages you to examine the congruence between your professed values and the choices you make in your daily life. How do your values manifest in your behavior, relationships, and pursuits? This exploration is a call to bridge the gap between intention and action, fostering a harmonious integration of values into your lived experience.

Defining Personal Identity: Unveiling the Tapestry of the Self

In the kaleidoscope of human existence, personal identity forms the intricate pattern that distinguishes us as individuals. It is the amalgamation of our experiences, beliefs, and relationships, creating a unique tapestry that unfolds with every moment. To embark on the journey of defining personal identity is to unravel the threads that compose the essence of who we are and understand the rich layers that shape our authentic selves.

Cultural Influences

Our cultural roots are a foundational aspect of our personal identity. This section prompts an exploration into the cultural tapestry that has woven itself into the fabric of your being. How have cultural influences shaped your values, perspectives, and traditions? This inquiry delves into the roots that anchor your identity in the diverse landscapes of heritage and tradition.

Journal Prompts:

Reflect on the cultural traditions and practices that were integral to your upbringing. How have they influenced your identity?

Consider a specific cultural value that holds significance for you. How does it manifest in your daily life and interactions?

Explore any conflicts or harmonies between your cultural identity and the broader societal context in which you live.

Roles and Identities

Beyond cultural influences, personal identity is also woven through the roles we inhabit. This section invites introspection into the various facets of your identity, whether as a friend, sibling, professional, or in any other role you play. How do these roles shape your sense of self, and how do you navigate the sometimes intricate interplay between them?

CHAPTER 4

WHAT DOES MENTAL TOUGHNESS ACTUALLY ENTAIL?

I'm frequently asked what I believe to be the key ingredients which make for optimal performance in any endeavor. These include the various academic and athletic activities for the most part. In truth, people already know the answer to this question. We all know that it takes a combination of both natural, physical ability, in addition to the mental capacity and drive to achieve success. This is acutely true for top level athletes, but the same can be said for being a great business leader or excellent parent for instance. The same rules apply. So the question really is, what percentage of these factors produces the best results?
Its no surprise that the person who is the most naturally gifted will typically come out ahead.

Although when these innate abilities are closely matched, the person with the right mindset will win every time. This is because the most in-depth studies show that physical talent and skill, only account for around 30% of peak performance. That leaves a whopping 70% for mindset and work ethic! A lot of ground can be made up with the correct thinking patterns and application in this sense.

I certainly don't doubt the impact our cognitive capabilities have over our real life results. My entire academic and working life has been dedicated to uncovering the most efficient psychological techniques and strategies in this regard. However, as I have already stated, I do not hold a main stream view on mental toughness. Why? I have simply seen it fail on too many occasions. Or work for a short period of time, but ultimately let the person down when it matters most. Short bursts of motivational activity or mental grit will fizzle out before long.

This is the official definition of mental toughness which everyone clings onto. It's the measure of individual resilience and confidence which can predict success in sport, education, workplace or any endeavor for that matter. I actually don't disagree with this entirely, as I do think resilience is an extremely important factor in terms of what a person will get out of life. But its how we get there which counts. I believe its achieved in a different way than you might imagine. Its not acquired through constant effort and struggle, but rather surrender. But more on this later.

Lessons From the Military

We traditionally get our notions on mental toughness from the professional service men and women around the world. These individuals have to attain high levels of mental and physical strength as must, not by choice. Brutal training regiments and boot camps are designed to push army, air force and navy cadets to the limit. To test their physical and mental capabilities, and continually push through them. These training camps are designed to break people down. To take their bodies, and more importantly the mind, to places they haven't been before. So when faced with similar situations in the field, they can handle them with ease.

We don't rise to the level of our expectations. We fall to the level of our training

This seems to confirm the studies I've already suggested, that the physical attributes, like speed, strength and cardiovascular endurance, aren't the things which determine results the most. Its the individuals ability to persist through the pain, in essence, its those with the greatest mental toughness who come out ahead. Its the ability to pick the body up and move it, even though you feel there's noting left in the tank.

Retired Navy Seal and ultra-endurance athlete David Goggins, is famous for stating that at the point of complete and utter physical exhaustion, the body is only around 50% of max output. Its up to the mind to push the arms and legs to squeeze out the additional 50% of potential. But very few of us will ever experience this level of physical training in reality. That's not to say we can't employ the same tactics to a lesser, more manageable degree. I am a big proponent of continually pushing yourself to expand the perimeters of your comfort zone.

My work has been focused on how best to do this for the everyday individual. In reality, its about defining what mental toughness means to the average person on the street. Pinpointing what it entails for you. This can be any variation of factors which may or may not include any of the following:

- Working out 4 days a week for an entire month
- Spending an hour with your kids each morning before school
- Completing work or college assignments on time
- Meditating for 30 minutes everyday

It doesn't matter what this maybe for you, you simply have to clearly define them. Mental toughness starts within the mind. It begins with the mental fortitude to get something done. But it also requires subsequent physical effort to complete the task or activity. Only then can you confirm its accomplishment. This requires definite action steps and goals to achieve. As we'll see later on, this comes through changing ingrained thought patterns and developing better habits by and large.

It entails changing the mental picture of yourself, visualizing the person who can get these things done with ease. This is how you achieve mental toughness without struggle. That is how you get the most done with minimal effort. I'm certainly not adverse to grafting hard when its required, but it just doesn't work when trying to overcome hurdles in your mind. For this, you need to follow the path of least resistance, and this comes from surrender.

This is the big lie we are fed in society. We are told that it takes 80 hour work weeks of blood, sweat and tears to get anything of significance done. Although, if you have ever witnessed truly high performance people at work, they seem to accomplish everything almost effortlessly. That is because they are not continually tripping themselves up in their mind. They have simply made the necessary adjustments in their thinking to produce the results they are getting. Hard work for hard works sake is a myth. If you are unsure of this, the following chapter will highlight some more examples to demonstrate this point more clearly.

CHAPTER 5

GETTING STARTED

Define a goal, this goal is like fuel in the tank of your car. Defining a goal gives you direction, what do want to accomplish? Why do you want it? Break down the goal into small parts, this gives you the ability to see a path from where you are to where you want to be.

Once you know where you want to go; and where you are, you can begin walking. Now I've found that it's best to set a goal for the year, big enough that it's gonna make you push your limits; but not so big that you get discouraged, or feel as though you can't accomplish it.

Breaking down the goal into small pieces, gives you the ability to easily work on it without feeling overwhelmed. Now I know that you're wondering, what do goals have to do with discipline? But its like this, to achieve goals you must be disciplined; and if you're disciplined you will achieve your goals! It's a positive feedback loop that you need to jump into, the jump will be hard, and scary but once you get in the waters nice.

I could never have done what I did without the habits of punctuality, order, and diligence, without the determination to concentrate myself on one subject at a time. – Charles Dickens

Make a plan, that you can follow to bring you closer to your end of year goal. Now it's easy to get carried away with this. You're not going to be good at first, relax and make a simple plan you can execute immediately.

As you go along, you will see ways to make your plan better and become more efficient. Start with a plan that you can execute immediately, and maintain with effort that's just out of your comfort zone. Remember you're building momentum to succeed, you don't want to get burnt out and give up.

Make sacrifices that will allow you to focus on your daily plan, which will take you to your goal, and stick with it! This is where the positive upward spiral starts, in a war against your weaker self, there will be many casualties.

Tv, social media, happy hour at the bar, these are just a few things you may need to sacrifice in order to commit to your goal, and in order to master self discipline. It's important not to go berserk though. I understand a lot of people need tv to help them disconnect.

But disconnecting is the problem, it's better to take the red pill and see what would happen if you don't give up, face your chores and responsibilities one day at a time in a manageable way; rather than to take that blue pill and plunge into the matrix of endless Netflix series.

You have to have a patience for exercise. You have to have a patience for college. You have to have a patience for relationships. Once the momentum gets going it takes on a life all of its
Simon Sinek

CHAPTER 6

KEYS TO SELF-DISCIPLINE

Every time the new year comes, it gives us the chance to start afresh or create new goals, get new accomplishments in our life and get rid of old habits, thoughts and issues that are holding us back. Self-discipline is the key to any success, health-wise, fitness -wise, and business-wise. It is 100% our efforts; you have to master it through consistency and persistence to follow through even when you feel you don't want to do it.

The cause of our lots of frustrations, sadness and disharmony with our relationships or personal level is lack of self-discipline, it is our inability to delay gratifications, seeing into our future how the decisions we take today will affect our future tomorrow, our inability to say no to additional obligations or responsibility, unwise spendings of our time, money and energy. It is not something you build overnight; you start building it with small little habits, something like a business call you have to make today, and you put it off for tomorrow, those books you want to read, and you keep postponing it.

This overtimes build debilitating insecurity within yourself; you no longer feel like that person that is true to your words and having to follow through. Simple things like keeping your house tidy and neat, your workspace clean, your clothes hanging them instead of having them clutter in your room, I am not saying you have to be obsessive or compulsive, but is just having that inner glow that you are self-disciplined and when you are disciplined in small task you then increase to more significant work. It becomes more natural in every part of your life as you start practising the art of self-discipline. People are looking for the spiritual magic pills that will make them feel better without making the necessary sacrifice needed, we want all the pleasurable things in life and don't want to reap the consequences. When you make self-discipline your focal point, you will notice that your energy is more centred within, is not being drained by chaos or problems in your life. You keep and harness your energy and spend it more productively in something you are passionate about like reading, writing, hiking, exercising or hanging out in nature. The human mind gravitates towards instant pleasure, and it takes a lot of self-discipline to rise above it.

UNDERSTANDING THE ESSENCE OF SELF-CONTROL

Self-control, the cornerstone of human behavior, testifies to our capacity for rational decision-making and emotional regulation. In the complex fabric of psychology, self-control emerges as a dynamic force that shapes our responses to myriad stimuli and manipulates the delicate balance between impulsive and rational behavior. In this course, we will get to the heart of self-control, explore its underlying principles, gain insights from key research in the field, and adopt an academic tone to examine the complexities that govern this fundamental aspect of human behavior.

The ability to put long-term objectives and values ahead of transient urges and temptations is the foundation of self-control. Researchers from a variety of fields have worked to understand the emotional and cognitive foundations of self-control as well as the mechanisms that allow people to put long-term objectives ahead of fleeting desires.

The Stanford Marshmallow Experiment, carried out by psychologist Walter Mischel and associates in the late 1960s and early 1970s, made a significant contribution to our understanding of self-control. Preschoolers were given the option to select between a smaller reward (like one marshmallow) that they could get right away and a bigger reward (like two marshmallows) if they waited a short while (usually 15 minutes). Children with better self-control during childhood demonstrated more positive life outcomes in terms of academic achievement, health, and social competence. The study also found that there were significant differences in children's ability to delay gratification.

On the basis of this foundational research, current neuroscientific investigations have shed light on the brain processes that underlie self-control. Impulse control is largely mediated by the prefrontal cortex, a brain region linked to executive function and decision-making. According to psychologist Walter Mischel's well-known hot and cold system model, self-control is the result of a dynamic interplay between an emotionally charged, impulsive hot system and a goal-oriented, contemplative cold system. The development of self-control leads to the appearance of a crucial tool. The key to developing self-control is the capacity to consider and assess one's own ideas, deeds, and motivations. This chapter examines useful techniques for self-reflection and acknowledges that it's a potent tool for developing one's own self-awareness and self-control.

According to psychologist Roy Baumeister and others, the strength model of self-control also makes the assumption that self-control is a limited resource that must be exhausted through effort. According to this model, temporarily decreasing one's overall capacity for self-control through self-control exercises like resisting temptation or making difficult decisions is referred to as ego depletion. Later studies have added to a more complex understanding of the complexities involved in self-control, while also providing support for and opposition to this model.

In addition to cognitive and neuroscientific perspectives, the socio-cultural dimensions of self-control cannot be ignored. Cultural norms, social expectations and individual differences contribute to variations in the expression of self-control in different contexts and populations. Research examining cultural differences in self-control has highlighted how cultural values and social norms shape individuals' perceptions of self-control and influence their behavioral responses to self-control challenges.

Moreover, the concept of self-control intersects with several areas of applied psychology, such as clinical psychology and behavioral economics. In a clinical context, understanding self-control is crucial for interventions targeting impulse control disorders, addictions and mental health problems.

Behavioral economics is a field that integrates findings from psychology and economics, investigating the decision-making processes underlying self-control in the domain of economic choice and shedding light on how individuals navigate complex trade-offs between immediate rewards and long-term economic goals.

After all, the intricate interaction of mental, emotional, and neurological processes shaped by social and cultural contexts is what ultimately constitutes self-control. The groundwork for comprehending the developmental trajectories and life outcomes linked to self-control has been established by significant research, such as Stanford University's Marshmallow experiment.

Contemporary research continues to explore the mechanisms and complexities underlying self-control, providing valuable insights into understanding human behavior and paving the way for targeted interventions in fields ranging from clinical psychology to economic decision-making. The journey to understand the nature of self-control continues, each study adding its own brush to the evolving portrait of this fundamental aspect of human nature.

The interplay between self-discipline and personal growth constitutes a profound journey through the human experience. As we navigate this complex landscape, the delicate balance between prudent self-control and unrestrained impulsivity emerges as a decisive force shaping destiny and influencing life.

CHAPTER 7

WHY YOU NEED TO BE SELF-DISCIPLINED

The mind represents the single, most important organ in the human body. Our mind controls our decisions, actions and ultimately our destiny through the kind of thoughts we hold in our mind. Our mind though is built to naturally seek out pleasure. For this reason, if you fail to harness your mind and milk it to produce the most effective and vital thoughts and decisions, you run the risk of being led on a fool's errand. If you fail to show discipline, you may run yourself into the ground without achieving the required results. What are the benefits of making the effort to be self-disciplined?

A vital component of success

Self discipline is an integral component of unbridled success. It can be quite hard to reach the goals you have in mind; it may be tough to satisfy the potential within you. There are so many potential obstacles that can negatively impact your will and desire to make the needed changes to succeed. Self discipline gives you an edge over these challenges. If at all, you cannot immediately overcome them, being disciplined can give you the fortitude to keep chipping away at them until there is a break in their structure. More people fail due to distractions than actual failures. Many people fail due to their own personal inability to stay true to their planned course of action than actually failing at the things they do.

Creates an identity for you

Everyone knows and identifies a disciplined person as a positive influence. Disciplined people always bring a difference to whatever they are doing. The discipline in them dictates that they hit certain standards each and every time they make an effort at something. Therefore, they come to be recognized for their unique and effective ways of getting things done. In fact, a vast majority of people while recognizing the effectiveness of self-discipline believe it is hard and tough to maintain some modicum of discipline. So, there is a healthy respect for anybody that can actually prove to be disciplined.

Sharpens your focus

Focus is very important. Forget the old saying of killing two birds with one stone. A large majority of the time, not deciding which particular stone is meant for each individual bird means that you are not going to even land a stone anywhere near any of the birds. Point-sharp focus is required to blur out distractions and potential energy-draining side attractions. With discipline, you learn to keep your eyes on the prize and forget about every other thing along the path. It will enable you get to your goal as quick as humanly possible.

Provides a clear map to the top

Have you ever driven around town without any specific destination in mind? If you have, how can you describe your movement pattern? Haphazard, undecided, rough, disorderly and directionless? Well, that is exactly what a life shorn of self-discipline looks like. Without discipline, you run the risk of simply running around life without a clear vision of where you want to be. But discipline not only shows you a clear destination, it hands you the map to the destination. All you have to do is maintain the path set out for you.

Helps others build trust in you

Self-discipline raises your stock in the eyes of associates, friends and relatives. When people have singled you out as being self-disciplined, they come to respect your ability to make the necessary sacrifices. They begin to appreciate the hard-work that you have put in to build up a reserve of discipline to tap into. They become much more willing to work with you as they know exactly what they are getting from associating with an individual with a well planned out life such as yours.

Teaches you perseverance

Perseverance is half of self discipline. Showing grit is one of the most desirable things a man can have. Being able to continue along the tunnel even when you have no idea if there is a light at the end, is a prime quality that can get you out of even the tightest of corners. Disciplined people find it easier to stick rather than turn at the first sign of trouble or problems arising. Knowing exactly what they want makes it easier for them to weather out the storms of adversities or perennial setbacks.

Protects you from rash and impulsive decisions

Impulsiveness is not a trait associated with successful minds. It is much more commonly found in people who have issues with sticking to their own plans. Instead, discipline makes sure every step you take is well thought out in advance and is a calculated progression in your pursuit.

Gets you motivated

With a clear line of sight to your route to the top, it is hard to not feel motivated when you have enough self-discipline. In fact, self-discipline itself is a product of your motivation to succeed. Therefore, a disciplined man is a motivated man.

Creates self-confidence

When you know exactly what you need to do, how to do it and are sure you are going to do it, you can afford to be secure in your own abilities and potential to cause the intended effects you want. You can afford to be bullish about your chances and walk around with real belief and a high level of esteem.

Keeps you in charge

Would you rather be a passenger or a driver in the vehicle of your destiny? Are you going to permit life to throw you around or are you going to take the wheels of your destiny and guide yourself to the exact place you want to be. Discipline gives you the chance to be more than just a spectator in your own life. Instead, it hands you the key to dictate where you want to go to.

An orderly routine

In hindsight, you are going to find out that your daily routine is much more important than you thought. Your routine is not only going to determine what happens today; it will in fact, determine to what extent your efforts are successful. Therefore, you cannot afford to have anything but the best possibly ordered routine, and self-discipline gives you the tools to set and maintain such a routine up.

CHAPTER 8

THE DISCIPLINED MINDSET

Integrating discipline into our lives isn't easy, truth be told, but so is integrating any kind of personal virtue.

This hardship lies within our mindsets, so in order to add discipline to your mind you must change more than your schedule. You must change the way you think.

So, how do you go about changing this?

The first thing you've got to add to your mindset is commitment: not only because discipline goes hand-to-hand with responsibility, but because you need to do *what you* have to do.

To become committed, you first need to understand the difference between a simple desire and an actual commitment. The first is... just that, you desire to do something so you do it whenever you can or if you feel like it. But, when you're committed, you do it without excuses, seeking only to produce results.

Think of being committed as being under a contract; when you commit yourself to something you enter into a binding pledge that forces you to carry out an appropriate course of action to achieve an end. To some, this whole idea seems exaggerated but commitment is something you must do in your life, both personally and professionally, in order to unleash your whole potential.

When you're committed, quitting or half-baking isn't a solution and neither is looking back or having second-thoughts when facing obstacles. Every time you pick something up; a project, a job, even a promise, you've got to convince yourself that you're committed to it. You need to push yourself to complete it, and if you get slightly out of the loop you must remind yourself I am committed to this.

The second thing you've got to add to your mindset is focus, and I can't stress hard enough just how important focus is in your life.

What do I mean by focus? Well, exactly that.

The center of interest or activity.

When we focus on something, we make that *something* our center of attention. However, there's another reason we use the word focus in this segment.

A point at which rays converge.

By metaphorical extent, when we focus, we direct *something* into a particular point. Focusing our efforts means directing all our strength and energy into achieving an end, and this is far more effective than spreading our efforts through a lot of things.

Imagine you had to bring down a wooden wall with a hammer and remove a door lock with a screwdriver. Surely you realize that the better approach would be directing all your strength into bringing down the wall with precise, careful strikes, and then unscrewing all the lock's screws patiently to detach it from the door. Imagine how time-consuming and tiresome it would be if you gave a spin to each screw, hit the wall once, went back to the lock, and kept repeating the whole cycle. You would take too much time doing that, wouldn't you?

The same logic applies in life. If you take on many activities at once, and you're not disciplined/organized/skilled enough, you will end up wasting your time and energy while getting sub par results.

Meanwhile, focusing all your strength into a single task not only warrants that you will get good results, but it warrants that it'll take less time (at least usually). So, the next time you find yourself taking up a task or a project, remind yourself that you're going to dump all your motivation and strength into getting it done before anything else.

The third thing you've got to add to your mindset is consistency, and this can be, in a way, regarded as the combination of commitment and focus.
 What do I mean by consistency?

Firmness of constitution or character.

Being consistent is synonymous with being perseverant. It means pushing forward without hesitation, without leaving things half-done just to pick another task that will surely suffer the same fate.

Try to recount about all the projects that you've undertaken through your life. Now, try to think how would your life be if you had persevered.

In a year, you're going to be wishing you had done what you promised yourself today, so you just have to remember that if you're not being consistent with your efforts, you're essentially wasting them.

Imagine that your goal is lifting a heavy stone resting on one side of a scale. No matter how light or heavy the weights you put in one side, if their combined weight isn't higher than the other side of the scale, you might as well have nothing there.

One of my favorite phrases for this is *almost doesn't count*; you either did something or you didn't. Some might add, you either do something well or not at all.

To be persistent, one has to focus one's efforts in the task one has committed to.

With these three elements looming in your head, you will open the doors for success, and in the process, you will become disciplined.

Please, try to internalize these three elements. In the following chapter, I will be giving you detailed habits that you can practice every day to become a disciplined, achieving, and effective, person.

CHAPTER 9

THE PSYCHOLOGY OF SELF-DISCIPLINE

Understanding the Inner Workings

Self-discipline is not merely a matter of willpower or self-control; it is deeply rooted in the psychology of human behavior. In this chapter, we will explore the underlying psychological principles that influence self-discipline and delve into the intricate workings of the human mind. By understanding the psychological factors at play, we can gain valuable insights into how to cultivate and strengthen our self-discipline.

The Role of Motivation

Motivation is the driving force behind self-discipline. It is the spark that ignites our desire to pursue our goals and overcome challenges.

Understanding the nature of motivation is crucial for developing sustainable self-discipline.

Intrinsic motivation, which stems from internal factors such as personal values and interests, is a powerful catalyst for self-discipline. When we are genuinely passionate about our goals, we are more likely to exhibit disciplined behavior consistently. On the other hand, extrinsic motivation, which arises from external rewards or punishments, may provide initial motivation but is less effective in sustaining long-term self-discipline.

To harness the power of motivation, it is important to identify our intrinsic motivations and align our goals with our core values. By connecting our aspirations to a deeper sense of purpose, we create a strong internal drive that propels us forward, even in the face of challenges.

The Impact of Beliefs and Mindset

Our beliefs and mindset shape our perception of ourselves, our abilities, and the world around us. They can either fuel or hinder our self-discipline efforts. Developing a growth mindset, which views challenges as opportunities for learning and growth, is essential for cultivating self-discipline.

Believing in our capacity to change and improve empowers us to persist in the face of setbacks. It enables us to view failures as stepping stones rather than roadblocks, leading to increased resilience and perseverance. By embracing a growth mindset, we can reframe obstacles as learning experiences and maintain a positive outlook on our self-disciplined journey.

Overcoming Procrastination

Procrastination is one of the most common barriers to self-discipline. It is the tendency to delay tasks or actions that require effort or discomfort in favor of immediate gratification. Understanding the psychological mechanisms behind procrastination can help us overcome this challenge.

Procrastination often arises from a fear of failure, perfectionism, or an inability to manage emotions and impulses effectively. By addressing these underlying factors, we can develop strategies to combat procrastination and enhance our self-discipline.

Setting clear and realistic goals, breaking tasks into manageable steps, and utilizing time-management techniques can help us overcome the allure of procrastination. Developing emotional regulation skills, practicing mindfulness, and creating an environment conducive to focus and productivity are also effective ways to combat procrastination and strengthen self-discipline.

Building Self-Awareness

Self-awareness is a cornerstone of self-discipline. It involves having a deep understanding of our thoughts, emotions, and behaviors, as well as their impact on our goals and aspirations. By cultivating self-awareness, we can identify the triggers and patterns that undermine our self-discipline efforts and make conscious choices to overcome them.

Journaling, meditation, and regular self-reflection are powerful tools for developing self-awareness. By examining our thoughts and emotions objectively, we can identify any self-limiting beliefs, negative self-talk, or emotional triggers that hinder our self-discipline. With increased self-awareness, we gain the ability to consciously redirect our thoughts, emotions, and behaviors toward disciplined actions that align with our goals.

The Power of Self-Reward and Accountability

Reward systems and accountability mechanisms play a vital role in cultivating and sustaining self-discipline. Humans are wired to seek rewards, and by leveraging this innate drive, we can reinforce disciplined behaviors.

Setting up a system of self-rewards for achieving milestones or completing tasks can be highly motivating. Celebrating small victories and acknowledging progress helps to create positive associations with disciplined actions, making them more likely to be repeated.

Furthermore, accountability can significantly enhance self-discipline. By sharing our goals and progress with trusted individuals, such as friends, family, or mentors, we create a sense of external responsibility. The knowledge that others are aware of our commitments helps to keep us on track and increases our self-discipline.

Understanding the psychology behind self-discipline is crucial for cultivating and strengthening this essential trait. By recognizing the role of motivation, beliefs, mindset, and self-awareness, we can develop effective strategies to overcome challenges such as procrastination and enhance our self-discipline.

In the following chapters, we will delve deeper into practical techniques and exercises that leverage psychological principles to bolster self-discipline. By applying these strategies, we will unlock the immense power of our minds and harness it to achieve lasting success.

CHAPTER 10

THE PRINCIPLES OF SELF-DISCIPLINE

Building a Solid Framework

Self-discipline is not a random act; it is guided by a set of fundamental principles that form the building blocks of this essential trait. In this chapter, we will explore the principles that underpin self-discipline and provide a solid framework for its cultivation and application. By understanding and embracing these principles, we can develop a strong foundation for our journey toward self-discipline.

Clarity of Purpose

Clarity of purpose is the first principle of self-discipline. It involves having a clear vision of what we want to achieve and a deep understanding of why it matters to us. When we have a compelling purpose that resonates with our values and aspirations, it becomes the driving force behind our disciplined actions.

To cultivate clarity of purpose, it is essential to reflect on our values, interests, and long-term goals. We must identify what truly matters to us and envision the impact we want to create in our lives and the lives of others. By aligning our actions with our purpose, we gain the motivation and focus needed to maintain self-discipline.

Goal Setting and Planning

Goal setting and planning are integral components of self-discipline. They provide a roadmap for our actions, breaking down our vision into specific, measurable, achievable, relevant, and time-bound (SMART) goals. Without clear goals and a well-thought-out plan, self-discipline can become aimless and ineffective.

To set effective goals, we must be specific about what we want to achieve, ensure our goals are realistic and attainable, and establish a timeline for completion. Breaking down larger goals into smaller, manageable steps helps to create a sense of progress and prevents overwhelm.

Planning involves mapping out the necessary actions, resources, and timelines required to achieve our goals. By developing a systematic plan, we enhance our self-discipline by providing structure, organization, and direction to our efforts.

Consistency and Commitment

Consistency and commitment are foundational principles of self-discipline. It is the unwavering commitment to taking disciplined actions consistently that leads to lasting success. Without consistency, self-discipline becomes sporadic and unreliable.

To cultivate consistency and commitment, we must establish daily routines and rituals that support our goals. By showing up consistently and dedicating time and energy to our disciplined actions, we build momentum and reinforce positive habits.

It is important to remember that self-discipline is a long-term commitment. It requires perseverance, even when faced with setbacks and challenges. Embracing the principle of consistency and maintaining our commitment to self-discipline enables us to overcome obstacles and stay the course.

Resilience and Adaptability

Resilience and adaptability are essential principles of self-discipline. They enable us to bounce back from failures, adjust our strategies when necessary, and navigate unexpected obstacles with grace and determination.

Resilience involves cultivating a positive mindset and viewing setbacks as learning opportunities. It is the ability to persevere and maintain our self-discipline even when faced with adversity. By developing resilience, we can weather the storms along our journey and emerge stronger and more determined than before.

Adaptability is the capacity to adjust our plans and approaches as circumstances change. It requires flexibility and openness to new ideas and strategies. When we encounter roadblocks or find that our initial plans are not yielding the desired results, being adaptable allows us to reassess, recalibrate, and find alternative paths to our goals.

Self-Care and Balance

Self-care and balance are often overlooked but crucial principles of self-discipline. It involves nurturing our physical, mental, and emotional well-being to ensure sustainable self-discipline.

Taking care of ourselves physically, through regular exercise, proper nutrition, and adequate rest, provides the energy and vitality needed for disciplined actions. Prioritizing our mental and emotional well-being, through practices such as mindfulness, relaxation techniques, and seeking support when needed, strengthens our resilience and mental clarity.

Additionally, maintaining a sense of balance in our lives is vital. It involves allocating time and energy to various aspects of our lives, including relationships, hobbies, and leisure activities. By maintaining a balanced lifestyle, we avoid burnout and sustain our self-discipline in the long run.

The principles of self-discipline provide us with a solid framework for cultivating and applying this vital trait. By embracing clarity of purpose, setting goals and planning, committing to consistency, cultivating resilience and adaptability, and practicing self-care and balance, we establish a strong foundation for our self-discipline journey.

In the following chapters, we will delve deeper into practical techniques and exercises that leverage these principles to enhance our self-discipline. By incorporating these principles into our lives, we will unlock our full potential and achieve the lasting success we desire.

CHAPTER 11

CONQUER YOUR MIND, CONQUER THE WORLD

You are here because you want to improve your life. You might want to focus more on the tasks you need to complete at work. You might feel that your life needs more of a balance between work, time with your family, friends, and time for yourself. You might also be here because you want to improve your mindset by focusing on your self-discipline. No matter why you choose this book, the first step to mastering your self-discipline is understanding and developing it. The first step in this process is to conquer your mind, allowing you to conquer your world.

When I talk about conquering your world, I mean the world around you—the parts of the world you can control. The pieces of this include your mind, emotions, and actions. You can't control what other people do, say, or think. However, you can control how you react to other people's attitudes and actions.

Understanding Self-Discipline

People often struggle with self-discipline because they must step out of their comfort zone to improve themselves. It is a working progress that you will focus on every day of your life. You won't be perfect at it every day, but you will always do your best, and this is exactly what you need to do. It is always important to take the success along with the failures as this shows your progress.

What Is Self-Discipline

Self-discipline is controlling your own thoughts, emotions, actions, and desires through self-improvement methods. The goal is that you will focus on developing your self-discipline by trying to better yourself every day. Learning self-discipline is not easy, but you will quickly notice the benefits and strive to better yourself in order to keep those benefits in your life.

Many people see self-discipline as an uneasy and difficult road to follow. As someone who has worked on developing self-discipline for years, I will admit it is not easy. There are days where you find yourself struggling more than most to stay in your disciplined mindset. However, once you gain the willpower, you will find a strategy that works for you. You will find yourself practicing self-discipline throughout your day. It will become a natural part of your routine.

Self-discipline is not denying yourself life's pleasures. It is not making sure you always walk in a straight line along your life's path. There are always bumps, curves, and even some potholes that you need to navigate, which might take you a bit off course. Self-discipline is a pleasant experience that you will find achievable. You will start to notice some of the benefits within days of working on your self-discipline, which will keep you more focused. In many ways, self-discipline is part of the puzzle of your life. Sometimes you lose the pieces, and you need to look for them. Sometimes they are right in front of your face, and other times it seems they fall from the sky and directly into place.

Self-discipline is one of the most important life skills for people to develop. Many people, especially those who have mastered self-discipline, compare it to a superpower because it allows you to remain mindful of your actions, thoughts, and emotions.

Mindfulness is when you are aware of everything going on in your environment — especially yourself. You notice if you ate enough, you know when you start to feel overwhelmed, when your thoughts are negative, or when you are tired and need to rest. Mindfulness and self-discipline go together. You cannot have one without the other.

This is because the opposite of mindfulness is mindlessness, which is when you are not aware of your environment, thoughts, emotions, and actions. Take a moment to think about driving your regular route to work, the grocery store, or your friend's house. You are used to the scenery and know exactly where you are going, so you let your mind wander. When you park your vehicle, you ask yourself how you got there because you don't remember part of the route. This is an example of becoming mindless. If you are mindful, you would remember everything about your drive.

Developing Your Self-Discipline

The most critical part of reaching your goals is developing your self-discipline. The struggle people tend to have is the resistance they feel, pulling them away from their self-discipline. For example, you started a new diet last week and are struggling to stay away from the food you love but can't have. Even though you threw away all the food in your home that you aren't allowed to eat on a diet, you continue to see the food everywhere. Potato chips, which are your favorite snacks, are not acceptable on this diet. You have been craving potato chips for several days and are not sure how much longer you can stay away from your favorite snack. Your mind keeps telling you, Just a few won't hurt you; buy a small bag and go for a long walk in the morning. After a few more days, you decide to have a cheat day and feed your cravings. You tell yourself, It will be better tomorrow. Besides, I have had a tough week, and everyone deserves a cheat day now and then.

The belief in cheat days leads people to lose their self-discipline when they start a diet. It is the thoughts you have that tell you, It is okay to have a few cookies, as long as you don't do it every day, that keep you from strengthening your self-discipline.

There are dozens of ways you can develop your self-discipline. You don't have to follow the path that other people have taken — you can develop your own plan and what works for your lifestyle and personality. In fact, you are more likely to succeed on your self-discipline journey if you develop your own path based on what you need.

Before I take you further into your self-development journey, you need to know these tips that will help you master your self-discipline.

Set clear goals.

One of the biggest reasons people struggle with self-discipline is because they do not establish clear goals. They have an idea of the goal they want to reach, but they don't think about the process of this goal. They don't form steps that will help them remain focused on their goals.

Create a backup plan.

A backup plan will help you through a difficult time or a moment when you find a fault in your original plan. Backup plans don't mean that you must stop focusing on your original plan. They simply mean that you will help yourself through the bumps in your path.

Know your weaknesses.

Your weaknesses are nothing to be ashamed of as everyone has weaknesses, just like everyone has strengths. The key is to understand your weaknesses, as this will guide you to know what direction you need to take on the path to reach your self-discipline. The only way you will overcome your weakness is by admitting you have them.

Keep your new habits simple.

Trying to follow a new habit can be a daunting task because it is hard to break your old habits. One way to keep yourself from feeling intimidated is to create simple new habits. For example, if you want to start working out for an hour every day to lose weight and get in shape, you will begin by exercising 15 minutes a day. Once you become more motivated to exercise, add 5 to 10 minutes to your time. Slowly increase your time until you are exercising for an hour a day.

Believe you have willpower.

When you believe you have willpower, you know you can achieve your goals. You will continue to build your motivation to succeed, which will increase your self-esteem and self-image. This will help you become a more positive person and continue to keep you motivated, even when you hit the bumps in the road.

Learn from your mistakes.

You will stumble from time to time, no matter how strong your self-discipline becomes. You can establish the best steps to reach your goals and still find yourself struggling. This happens to everyone, and it is important not to let it get you down. Acknowledge what happened and continue to move forward. When you start letting yourself feel angry or guilty, you will continue to struggle and slow down your progress. You can't succeed without failure.

Reward yourself.

One of the important steps in establishing your goals is making sure you set rewards for yourself. You want to treat yourself in a way that will keep you motivated to continue. For example, you might watch an episode of your favorite show on Netflix, go to the movies with a friend, or go out to eat.

Self-Confidence Vs. Self-Esteem

As an entrepreneur, Roger has recently learned he needs to work on self-improvement by taking control of his self-discipline. A couple of months ago, Roger started his own writing business, where he works for several clients as a writer and editor. Recently, Roger started to notice that he is not following his schedule, he is easily distracted, and he doesn't always have the willpower to sit at his desk and work. Roger knows that he doesn't lack the motivation for his work or lost interest in his job. He enjoys writing and has put in a lot of work over the last few years to establish his business.

Roger first realized his struggles getting into his schedule within his first week of working from home. At this time, Roger contributed his struggles to years of stress working two jobs. Not only did Roger focus on developing his business, but he also worked full-time as a journalist. His job often caused him to work more than 40 hours a week and odd hours to cover evening and weekend events. It caused him to lack a schedule with both jobs.

Furthermore, Roger worked close to 100 hours a week for over six months. These factors made Roger think he was dealing with the aftereffects of eliminating a huge amount of stress from his shoulders. He talked to His friends about his struggles, and they agreed that in a couple of weeks, Roger would start to focus more on his schedule and continue to build his business. But, almost two months later, Roger is still struggling. Roger has an idea of what self-discipline is but doesn't have a clear idea of effectively reaching self-discipline. He has never focused on improving his self-discipline and is unsure of the steps he will need to take. Roger starts to research self-discipline and incorporate its strategies into his life to have more motivation to follow his schedule and complete his tasks. The first point Roger learns is that he is already improving because he understands that he needs to work on his self-discipline. Roger is already improving because he acknowledges his weaknesses and focuses on establishing good self-discipline strategies to continue to grow his business and general self-improvement.

One of the first factors Roger realized about himself is his low self-confidence. He didn't realize all the negative thoughts he had throughout the day. He didn't notice how often he questioned his abilities as a writer and editor. Even though his clients loved his work, he continued to believe that his talent could vanish in an instant. He felt that his clients would find someone better, and his business would fail. Roger realized that he needed to change his mindset to gain a stronghold of his self-discipline.

One day at a time, Roger started building his plan to control his emotions and thoughts. He used strategies to become more mindful and started reflecting on his day by journaling for 15 minutes before going to bed. In the morning, he got up a half-hour early and started to meditate before getting ready for the day. He started to eat healthier, focusing on smaller meals and eating more often. Roger started snacking on healthy foods over cookies, chips, and candy. He gave up soda, started drinking more water, and got at least 7 hours of sleep every night. Over time, Roger started to feel better emotionally, mentally, and physically.

Like Roger, you don't think about self-discipline because you become comfortable with your daily routine and habits. They become a part of your life, and that is just the way it is. Another reason you don't spend a lot of thought on self-discipline is because of your low self-confidence.

It is important to understand the difference between self-confidence and self-esteem. You can have high self-esteem and still have low self-confidence. Your self-esteem is how you feel about yourself overall. You focus on the positive experiences that have happened throughout your life, giving you a positive outlook. Self-confidence is how you feel about your abilities and talents. You might think that your artwork or writing is never good enough or that you aren't good at math. However, you will feel that you are strong in other areas, such as interior decorating. Self-confidence can change from one situation to the next.

When you start observing yourself in the mission to increase your self-discipline, you will notice that you have high self-confidence where your self-discipline is strong. When your self-discipline is weak, your self-confidence is also weak. Your self-discipline follows how confident you feel about certain situations. To help you understand, think about a skill you feel you aren't good at. How motivated are you when it comes to focusing on that skill? For example, if you feel you aren't a good artist, you won't spend a lot of time drawing or painting. But, if your confidence is high as an artist, you are often motivated to work on your projects. If you need to, take some time to write down skills you are confident about and skills where your self-confidence is low. Then, take a moment to think about how motivated you are to focus on these skills. Write down how you feel about the skills and think of ways to start to build your self-confidence, thus building your self-discipline in these skills.

You need to remember that self-discipline is a skill, which is something that you learn over time. Developing your self-discipline takes time, patience, and commitment. You will find yourself feeling like you can't build your self-discipline, and you will have days where you are strong in this area of your life. Everything you feel as you work towards strengthening your self-discipline is normal. In the moments where you start to question yourself, take a moment to think about what you have accomplished. Above all, you always need to remember that you are on the right path and do a great job. You are not alone in this struggle. Always be proud of your improvements.

CHAPTER 12

THE SELF-DISCIPLINE FRAMEWORK

DEVELOPING A UNIQUE FRAMEWORK

Just as every fingerprint is distinct, so too should be your self-discipline framework. In this section, we'll dive into the art of crafting a framework that's tailored to your individual context and aspirations. Drawing from my own experiences as a medical student and doctor and my interactions with a diverse range of clients, I've witnessed the power of personalizing self-discipline strategies.

Imagine constructing a house; there's a blueprint, right? However, the final design is heavily influenced by the surroundings, available materials, and the owner's preferences. Similarly, your self-discipline framework should consider your environment, your strengths, and your unique goals.

In my medical journey, I crafted a framework that incorporated focused study sessions interspersed with moments of relaxation to optimize productivity. It wasn't a rigid schedule but a flexible structure that allowed me to maintain self-discipline while navigating the rigorous curriculum of medical school. This approach recognized the ebb and flow of my energy levels and the necessity of balance.

However, it's crucial to note that self-discipline isn't limited to the medical field. In my work with diverse clients, I've learned that a one-size-fits-all approach doesn't work. Each individual faces a unique set of challenges and aspirations, whether related to improving physical health, enhancing business ventures, or achieving personal milestones. For instance, I've coached clients aiming to enhance their physical fitness. Rather than prescribing a generic regimen, I've assisted them in developing personalized self-discipline frameworks that consider their specific circumstances. This process involves a deep understanding of their lifestyle, work commitments, and individual preferences. The result is a plan that harmonizes with their unique context, ensuring that self-discipline is both achievable and sustainable.

The key takeaway from this section is that your self-discipline framework is not a static template but a dynamic tool that should adapt to your evolving needs and circumstances. By recognizing the importance of personalization, you can craft a framework that harmonizes with your goals, your environment, and your strengths.

Balancing Motivation and Self-Discipline

In the realm of self-discipline, there's a dynamic interplay between motivation and self-discipline, and it's essential to strike a delicate balance. This section delves into the art of maintaining equilibrium between these two driving forces, drawing from my experiences as a medical student and doctor, as well as my interactions with a diverse range of clients.

Motivation is like the wind in your sails, providing that initial push, but it can be fickle. Self-discipline, on the other hand, acts as the rudder, steering you toward your goals, even when motivation wanes. Balancing these two elements is the key to consistent progress.

In the rigorous world of medicine, where the journey is long and demanding, motivation can ebb and flow. There were moments during my medical school years when the initial enthusiasm waned, and the path ahead seemed arduous. In such times, self-discipline was the steadfast companion that kept me on course.

The lesson here is that motivation is not always at its peak, but self-discipline can fill in the gaps. It's about understanding that motivation is ephemeral, while self-discipline is a steady force. Motivation can get you started, but it's self-discipline that keeps you going, even when the going gets tough.

In my work with clients, I've found that this balance between motivation and self-discipline is a universal concept. Take, for instance, clients aiming to enhance their physical fitness. At the outset, motivation is typically high, but it's common for this initial enthusiasm to wane over time. In such cases, we draw from the well of self-discipline, emphasizing the importance of consistent effort, even when motivation dips.

The key takeaway from this section is that self-discipline and motivation are not opposing forces but complementary partners in your journey. Motivation provides the initial impetus, but self-discipline ensures the journey continues, whether the motivation is present or not.

Measuring and Tracking Progress

Just as a ship uses navigational instruments to chart its course, you too can employ metrics to measure and track your self-discipline progress. In this section, we'll explore the importance of measuring and monitoring your journey.

Consider the example of a client embarking on a fitness journey. Setting specific, measurable goals is essential for tracking progress. We establish metrics like weight, body composition, and workout performance. These metrics serve as signposts on the path, helping us stay aligned with our goals.

Measuring and tracking progress is not limited to the realm of fitness; it applies to every facet of life. Whether you're aiming to reach professional milestones, maintain a healthy lifestyle, or achieve personal aspirations, metrics can be your guiding light.

In my medical journey, as I prepared for board exams and clinical rotations, progress metrics were crucial. We measured our understanding of medical concepts through practice exams, tracked our clinical skills development during rotations, and monitored our overall academic performance. These metrics were vital for making informed decisions and adjustments to our study strategies.

The power of metrics lies in their objectivity. They provide a clear picture of where you stand and whether you're moving in the right direction. When you track your progress, you can identify areas that require improvement and celebrate milestones along the way.

Moreover, metrics allow you to adapt your strategies. If you're not progressing as expected, it's a sign that something needs adjustment. In my work with clients, this adaptability has proven invaluable. We modify fitness routines, refine business strategies, and fine-tune personal development plans based on the metrics we've established.

The key takeaway from this section is that metrics are your allies in self-discipline. They offer a realistic perspective on your journey, helping you navigate with precision. Whether you're scaling the heights of professional success or pursuing personal growth, metrics provide the insights needed to stay on course and adjust your strategies as needed.

CHAPTER 13

MASTERING SELF-DISCIPLINE: THE FOUNDATION OF LASTING SUCCESS

Understanding Self-Discipline: More than Just Willpower

Imagine standing at the base of a majestic mountain. Its towering peak pierces the sky, and the path leading to the summit is filled with challenges: sharp rocks, treacherous turns, and steep inclines. Now, imagine two climbers. The first is filled with fiery passion and a burst of motivation to reach the peak. He starts quickly, driven by his excitement, but his energy quickly fades. After a short distance, he feels overwhelmed and decides that the climb is too difficult, and he abandons his quest.

The second climber, on the other hand, approaches the mountain with a calm determination. He has prepared both mentally and physically for the climb, understanding that it won't be easy. Each step is measured, and when he encounters obstacles, he pauses, reassesses, and finds a way forward. His journey is not fueled by mere momentary motivation but by a deep-rooted discipline that keeps him going, step by step, until he finally stands victorious at the summit.

In life, it is this enduring self-discipline that propels us forward. Willpower may ignite the initial spark, but without discipline, the journey is seldom completed. So let us cultivate discipline; let us be the second climber, who triumphs in the face of challenges and reaches new heights.

The Misconception of Willpower

In the popular imagination, willpower is often viewed as the ultimate determinant of those who achieve their goals and resist distractions or temptations. We've all heard phrases like, It's a matter of willpower, or, If only I had more willpower. This kind of thinking attributes a substantial portion of our success or failure in various endeavors, be it dieting, studying, or even saving money, to this singular, mysterious force. But is willpower truly the key? And if so, how does it operate? Let's explore the intricate dynamics surrounding willpower, its limitations, and the broader spectrum of factors that influence self-control.

Defining Willpower: A Comprehensive Perspective

Before delving deeper into the concept of willpower, it is essential to clarify that it plays a vital role in regulating our impulses, emotions, desires, and actions. Our ability to delay gratification, resist temptations, and pursue long-term goals, even when immediate rewards beckon, depends on it.

Its strength goes beyond mere determination. It's a complex interplay of various factors like cognitive abilities, emotional intelligence, energy levels, motivation, habitual patterns, and the cultural context. Mastering each of these dimensions can set the stage for significant breakthroughs in personal growth and attainment.

The Finite Model of Willpower

Willpower, in recent scientific studies, has been likened to a finite resource, similar to a muscle that can tire out after intense exertion. Similarly, our willpower can wane after periods of sustained mental effort or resistance to temptation, a phenomenon called ego depletion.

For instance, in a well-known experiment, participants who restrained themselves from the temptation of freshly baked cookies, subsequently showed reduced persistence in solving challenging puzzles. Their previous act of restraint had, it seems, drained their willpower. This example leads to a glucose-depletion effect, where glucose, a primary source of energy for the brain, decreased as participants exerted self-control.

What's fascinating is that this depletion seems to have a biological correlate. As participants exerted self-control, their glucose – a primary source of energy for the brain – levels decreased. When they replenished their glucose, their willpower also appeared to be restored.

Moreover, glucose's role is significant but more nuanced, intertwined with our beliefs about willpower, motivations, and overall physiological state. Therefore, simply downing a sugar-laden drink won't instantly supercharge one's willpower.

Beyond the Finite Model: Mindset, Motivation, and Other Elements

The muscle analogy and glucose observation are compelling, but they are only parts of a complex picture. Other research suggests that our beliefs about willpower can shape its reality, where those who perceive willpower as an inexhaustible resource tend to exhibit more stamina while requiring self-control than those who see it as finite. Additionally, motivation plays a colossal role, where pushing through even when our willpower reserves seem low becomes more attainable if the reasons for a task align deeply with our values or when there's substantial intrinsic motivation.

Moreover, while willpower is undoubtedly a crucial player in self-control, it doesn't operate in isolation. Several other elements come into play:

Habits: Once a behavior becomes habitual, it requires significantly less willpower. For example, someone who has cultivated the habit of running every morning might do so with little to no conscious effort.

Environment: Our surroundings have a profound effect on our behavior. A clutter-free workspace might enhance productivity, while a kitchen stocked with unhealthy snacks can thwart dieting efforts.

Support Systems: Having a support system, be it friends, family, or support groups, can act as external enforcers of discipline.

Mindset: A growth mindset, where challenges are seen as opportunities for growth rather than threats, can make perseverance more natural.

Rest and Recovery: Just as with physical exercise, periods of rest allow for the recovery of willpower. Sleep, relaxation, and leisure are vital.

Strategies for Enhancing Willpower

Given its importance and the challenges in maintaining it, are there ways to enhance our willpower? Yes, and they often lie in addressing the broader ecosystem of self-control.

Regularly challenge yourself: Much like a muscle, regular challenges, even small ones, can help in bolstering willpower.

Mindful practices: Activities like meditation can increase self-awareness, allowing for better impulse control.

Positive visualization: Visualizing the benefits of achieving a goal can provide a boost when willpower wanes.

Avoid decision fatigue: Reduce trivial decisions to preserve willpower for more critical tasks. For example, having a set routine or a predetermined menu can help.

In conclusion, understanding the intricacies of willpower, addressing the vast array of other factors at play, and taking the necessary steps to enhance it through a holistic approach may offer a more comprehensive perspective towards achieving greater success.

The Misconception of Willpower: A New Perspective

As we have seen therefore, recent research has shown that relying solely on willpower is like sprinting in a marathon race. Just as our physical energy diminishes, so does our willpower when continually taxed. Therefore, it is crucial to understand what makes up the fabric of self-discipline.

The Pillars of Self-Discipline

If we can't solely rely on willpower, what then makes up the fabric of self-discipline? Here are the integral pillars:

Awareness: The cornerstone of discipline is understanding one's strengths, weaknesses, desires, and triggers. Being acutely aware allows one to preempt challenges and strategize effectively.

Consistency: Unlike the sporadic nature of willpower, consistency ensures that actions become habits. It's not about monumental changes but small, daily actions that culminate in success.

Resilience: Discipline involves facing setbacks head-on and having the fortitude to bounce back, learning from each experience.

Prioritization: Not every task demands your attention. Knowing what aligns with your goals and dedicating time and effort to them is pivotal.

Delayed Gratification: At its core, discipline is about forgoing immediate pleasures for long-term gains. It's the ability to see beyond the present moment and work towards a future reward.

Harnessing the Power of Habit

Habits aren't just actions, as Charles Duhigg says in his renowned book The Power of Habit, but cycles that start with a cue, which leads to a routine and culminates in a reward. Understanding and manipulating this cycle is crucial in fostering discipline. A particular habit ingrained in our routine no longer relies on willpower; instead, it becomes a part of our muscle memory. For example, consider a practiced pianist. Their fingers glide over the keys, not because of daily bouts of motivation, but because disciplined practice has ingrained the movements into their very being.

The Path Ahead

The subsequent chapters offer a more detailed exploration of self-discipline, from its psychological foundations to its practical applications. Discipline is not about being stringent or restrictive; it is about harnessing an internal power, channeling it effectively, and cultivating a life where dreams are attainable realities. Understanding the terrain is the first step towards transforming your life with self-discipline.

The Impact of Self-Discipline on Life Success

There is a prevalent belief in our society that natural talent, luck, or even socioeconomic background are the predominant factors in achieving success. Despite the common perception, self-discipline is often the determining factor for long-term success. Self-discipline acts as a rudder in the vast ocean of life, allowing individuals to navigate storms, avoid pitfalls, and steer towards their desired destination.

The Domino Effect of Discipline

Imagine a line of dominoes. The act of pushing just one can set off a cascade, resulting in a spectacular display. Similarly, one disciplined action in life can trigger a series of beneficial events, creating an upward spiral of positive outcomes. For example, a commitment to waking up early can lead to a more productive morning routine, allowing for focused work, regular exercise, and a balanced breakfast. This series of disciplined actions contributes to better mental clarity, improved health, and enhanced overall well-being.

In other words, contrary to popular belief, success isn't always achieved through monumental decisions or grand gestures. Instead, it's a culmination of numerous small choices made through consistent, disciplined actions. These choices compound over time, leading to significant life successes.

Discipline as a Bridge to Turning Dreams into Reality

Everyone has dreams. But without discipline, dreams often remain just that - intangible and unrealized. By consistently applying effort towards achieving goals, individuals can turn their dreams into reality. For example:

Career Advancement: Those with discipline often stand out in the workplace. Their dedication to tasks, time management, and continual learning make them valuable assets, leading to opportunities for advancement and growth.

Health and Fitness: Disciplined habits such as balanced nutrition, regular exercise, and adequate sleep translate to robust health, reduced illness, and greater longevity.

Financial Security: Discipline in financial management, which includes saving, investing wisely, and curbing impulse purchases, paves the way for a stable financial future.

Creating Strong Relationships through Discipline

At a glance, discipline might seem unrelated to interpersonal relationships. However, a deeper look reveals its profound impact. By practicing self-discipline, individuals cultivate qualities like patience, active listening, and commitment, which strengthen bonds, build trust, and nurture enduring personal and professional relationships.

The Long-Term Vision

Through deliberate, disciplined growth, individuals can witness profound transformations in both their internal and external lives within a year. Mapping out a clear plan for the year, with quarterly reviews, monthly focus areas, weekly check-ins, and daily habits, provides the foundation for success. Consistent effort, embracing challenges, building a support system, documenting the journey, and celebrating milestones, no matter how small, are key in achieving a year of transformation.

Self-discipline promotes a forward-thinking mindset. Rather than being swept up in the immediacy of life's daily grind, disciplined individuals keep their eyes on the horizon. They set long-term goals and chart out pathways to reach them. This vision not only guides their current actions but also instills a sense of purpose and direction in life. With the tools of self-discipline in hand, individuals are poised to take on any journey, one day at a time, and achieve greatness.

The Journey Ahead: One Year of Dedicated Transformation

The ticking of a clock, the turning of calendar pages, the changing of seasons—time is ceaseless in its march. Yet, how we choose to utilize this time can drastically alter its significance in our lives. By dedicating ourselves to transformation, significant changes can be achieved in just one year, both internally and externally. This guide presents a clear path to deliberate and disciplined growth.

Creating a 365-Day Blueprint

Before beginning any journey, it's essential to have a clear plan. Breaking the year down into quarterly reviews, monthly focus areas, weekly check-ins, and daily habits ensures progress towards your goals.

This doesn't mean plotting out every single day to the last detail, but rather setting clear milestones and objectives. In the next chapters we will see together how to do it.

The Power of Consistency

In a world obsessed with overnight successes, the quiet power of consistency often goes unnoticed. Yet, it's in the daily grind, the unwavering commitment to the task at hand, that true transformation lies. Within a year, consistent effort can yield astounding results, from mastering a new skill to achieving a long-desired goal.

Embracing Challenges

Obstacles during your transformational journey are inevitable. There will be days of doubt, moments of weakness, and periods of stagnation. However, by facing these challenges head-on, you can grow both personally and professionally, furthering your progress and fortifying your character.

Building a Support System

Nobody can achieve their goals alone. Surrounding yourself with communities and mentors who align with your vision can prove invaluable in providing support, guidance, and shared experiences that can be invaluable. Remember, the power of collective energy and wisdom can significantly amplify individual efforts.

Documenting the Journey

Maintaining a journal or log of your progress offers a tangible record of achievements, while also serving as a motivator on days when your motivation wavers. Revisiting your documented journey can reignite the spark and remind you of how far you've come.

Celebrating Milestones, No Matter How Small

Acknowledging and cherishing every small triumph in your expedition can serve as a catalyst to propel you towards future successes. This gesture of recognition not only elevates your spirits quintessentially but also instills an unwavering drive to face any trials ahead.
The recognition and celebration of minor achievements play a critical role in the pursuit of larger goals. Often, we overlook the smaller milestones along the way. However, these seemingly insignificant accomplishments form the bedrock of ultimate success, and their acknowledgment can serve as a powerful

motivator. Every grand journey is made up of countless small steps. When we take the time to acknowledge each of these steps, we not only validate the hard work involved but also create a reinforcing loop. This affirmation boosts our self-confidence, reminding us of our capabilities and the progress we've made so far.

Furthermore, it helps to cultivate a mindset of gratitude and positivity. This attitude fosters resilience, particularly during challenging times when larger goals seem elusive. These moments of recognition provide mini-respites, allowing us to recharge and push forward with renewed vigor.

Consistently noting and celebrating minor accomplishments also creates a record of success over time. Reflecting on this growing list of achievements can provide the encouragement needed to overcome obstacles, ensuring that we remain motivated and committed to our overarching objectives. In essence, the recognition of small victories is not just a nod to the past but a potent catalyst for future endeavors.

In Conclusion

We often underestimate what we can do in a year. Through disciplined action, unwavering commitment, and a clear vision, 365 days can morph into a transformative expedition, reshaping the contours of one's life.
With this potential, it's a journey worth embarking upon. As the year begins, take up the challenge of crafting your masterpiece, one day at a time.
Importantly, while January is typically associated with new beginnings, personal growth and transformation aren't restricted to the start of the year. Any point on the calendar can be the

perfect time to embark on a journey of self-improvement. This guide offers monthly reflections and exercises to aid you on your path, but don't be afraid to customize them to fit your unique story. However, adhering to the recommended order will provide structure for those seeking guidance. Remember, having a roadmap - even if you diverge from it at times - is better than navigating solely by intuition.

CHAPTER 14

EMOTIONAL INTELLIGENCE

Recognizing Emotions: The Journey to Emotional Awareness

In the intricate landscape of human experience, emotions serve as the vibrant colors that paint the canvas of our lives. Recognizing and understanding these emotions is a key aspect of emotional intelligence, fostering a deeper connection with oneself and others. This section invites you to embark on a journey of self-discovery, exploring the nuances of your emotions and unraveling the threads that weave the tapestry of your inner world.

Emotion Identification

The first step on this journey is to hone the skill of identifying your emotions accurately. This involves going beyond simple labels and delving into the complex interplay of feelings that shape your daily experiences. Through mindful observation, you can cultivate a more nuanced understanding of the emotions that color your world.

Triggers and Responses

Understanding the triggers that elicit specific emotions and your responses to them is a crucial aspect of emotional intelligence. This section prompts you to explore the roots of your emotional responses, shedding light on the patterns and dynamics that influence your reactions.

Emotional Regulation: Nurturing Harmony Within

In the ebb and flow of life's emotional currents, the art of emotional regulation emerges as skillful navigation, allowing us to ride the waves with resilience and grace. This section invites you to explore the ways in which you can regulate and manage your emotions, fostering a balanced and empowered approach to the myriad feelings that color your experiences.

Coping Strategies

Amidst the cacophony of emotions, coping strategies serve as the tools in your emotional toolkit, enabling you to respond to challenges with resilience. This exploration encourages you to identify and cultivate effective coping mechanisms that align with your values and promote well-being.

Embracing Emotional Growth

Emotional regulation is not only about managing difficult emotions but also about embracing the potential for growth and self-discovery within each emotional experience. This section encourages you to view emotions as valuable messengers, guiding you toward personal evolution.

www.ingramcontent.com/pod-product-compliance
Lightning Source LLC
LaVergne TN
LVHW010216070526
838199LV00062B/4608